INSTRUCTIONS:

1. Think about the person you are making a card for.
2. Choose a card that you think will be perfect for that person.
3. Use colored pencils to color the card.
4. Use Scissors to cut out the card and envelope.
5. Use a glue stick to make your envelope.
6. Put the card inside the envelope and give it to someone you love!

Original Art by: Notika Pashinko

Cover By: Sarah Janisse Brown

The Thinking Tree, LLC   Copyright 2017   Do Not Copy

FunSchoolingBooks.com

Some pages are blank so you can add your own designs to the insides of the cards and envelopes.

Some pages are blank so you can add your own designs to the insides of the cards and envelopes.

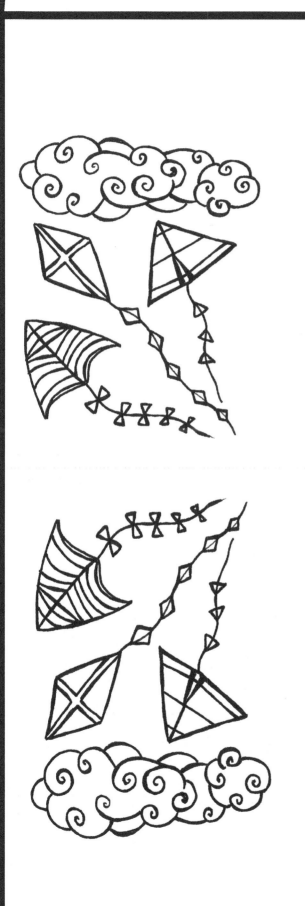

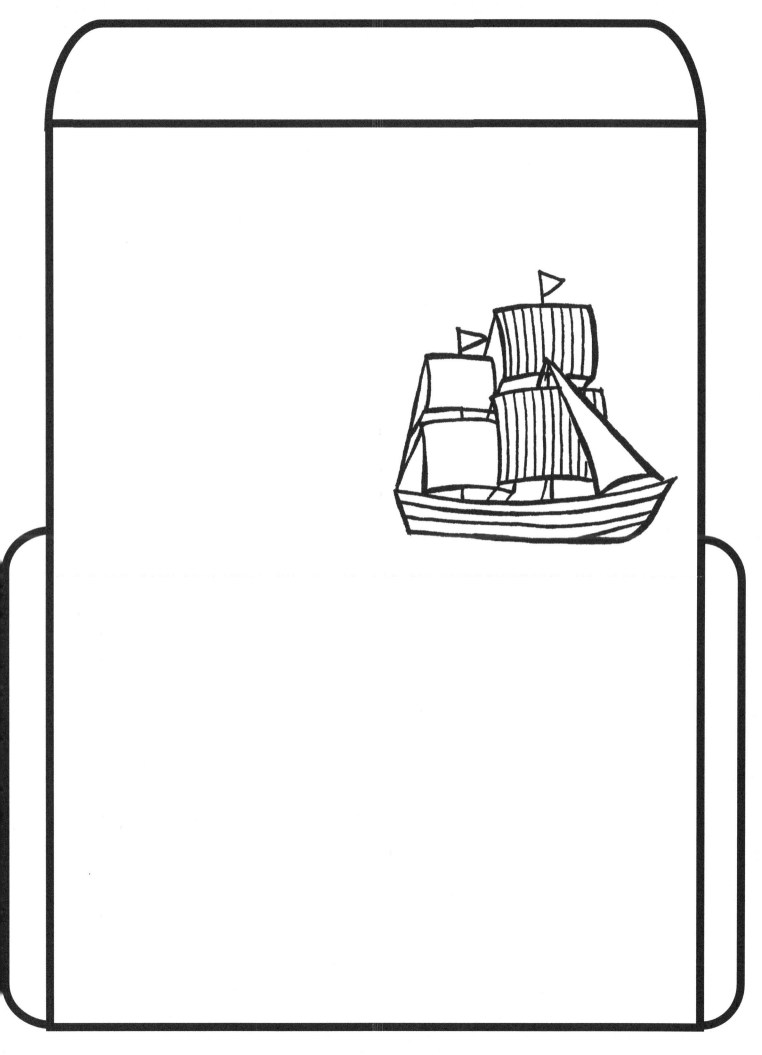

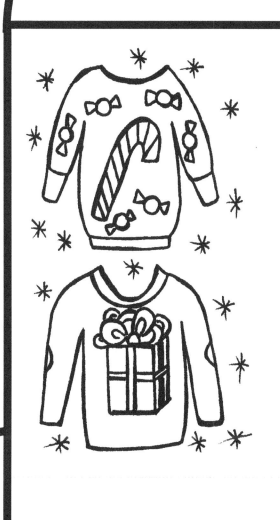

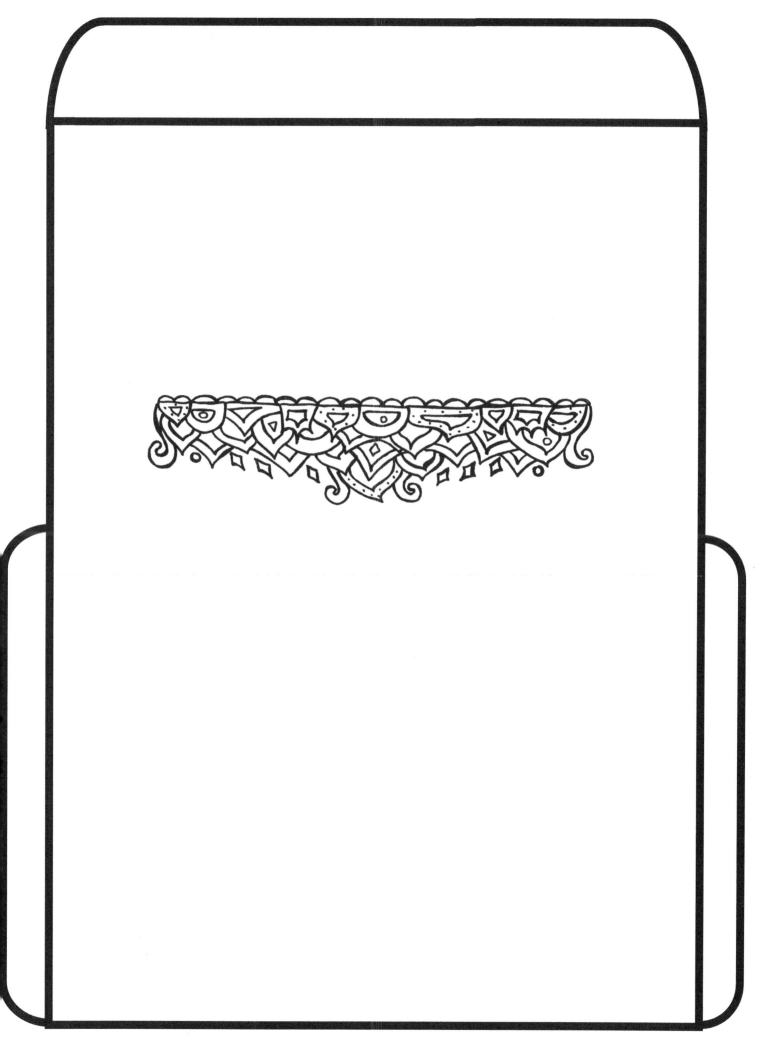

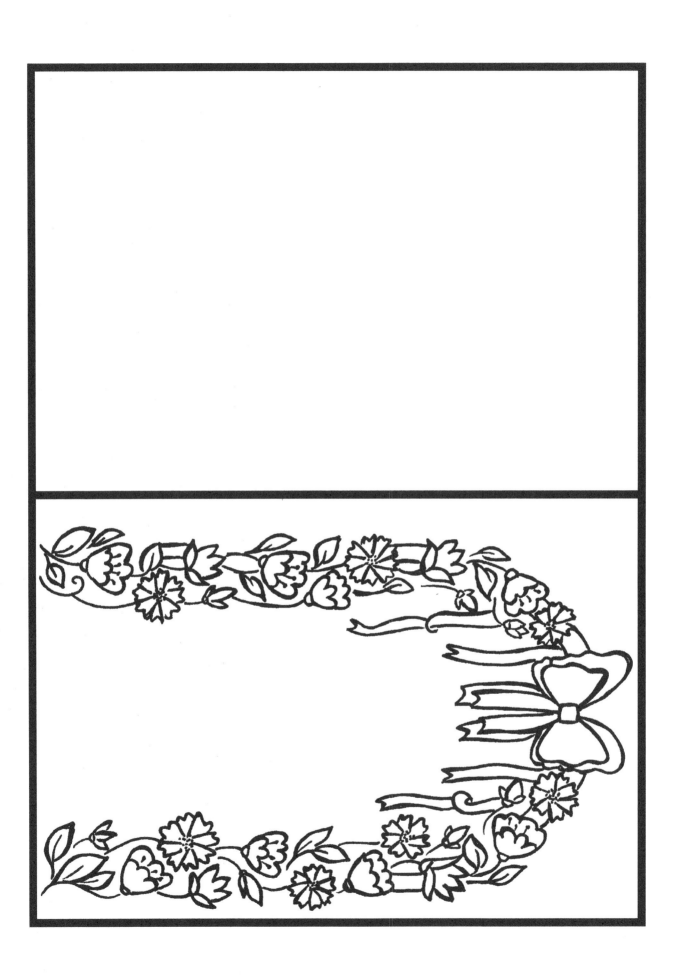

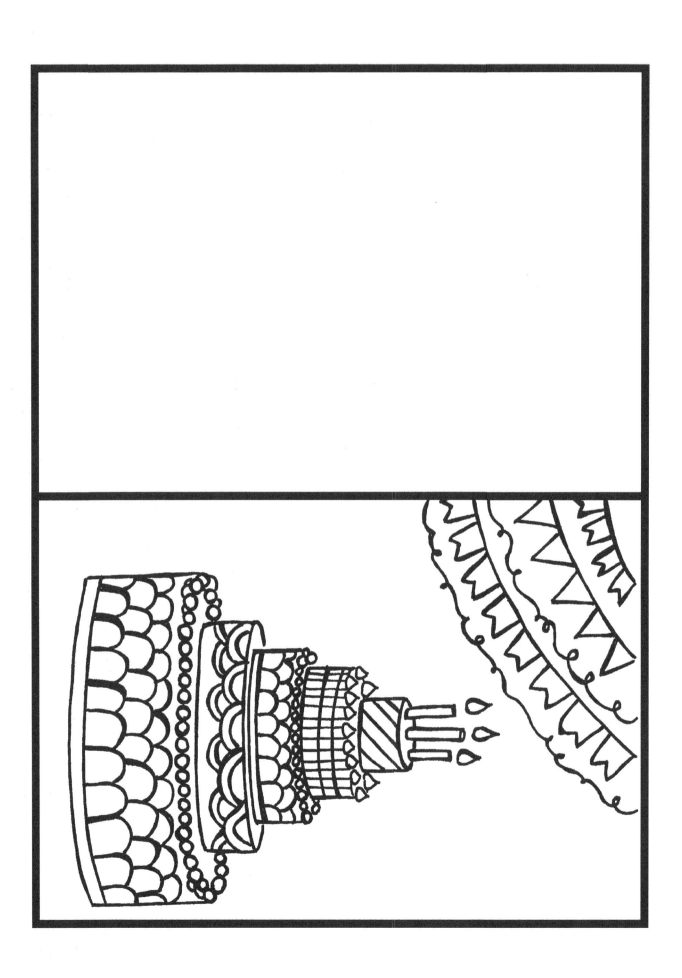

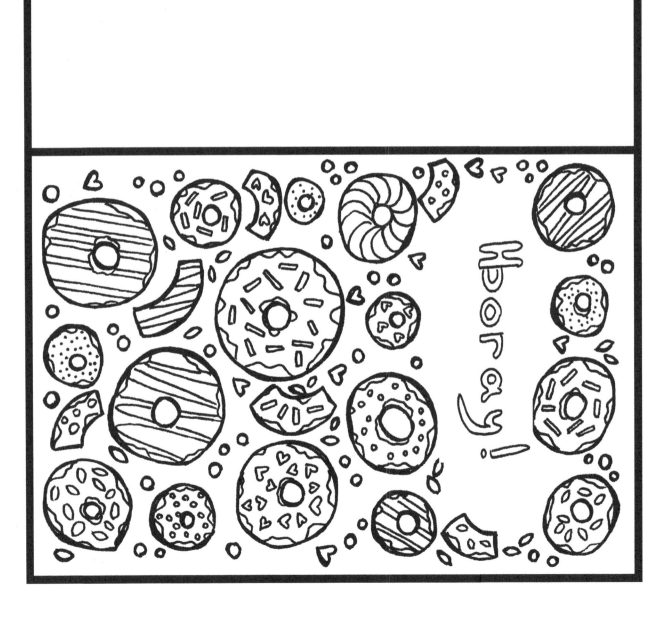

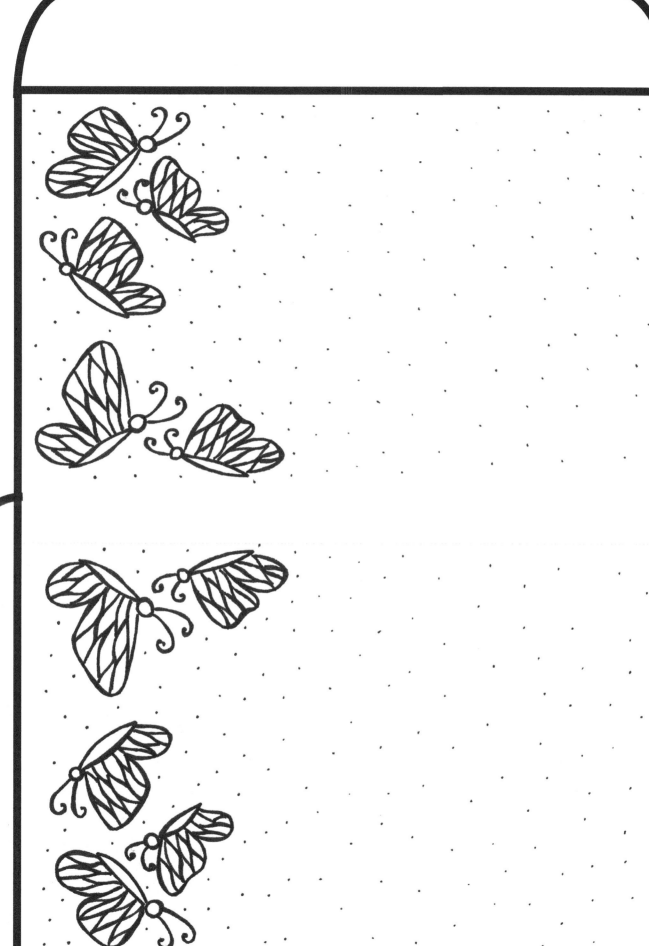

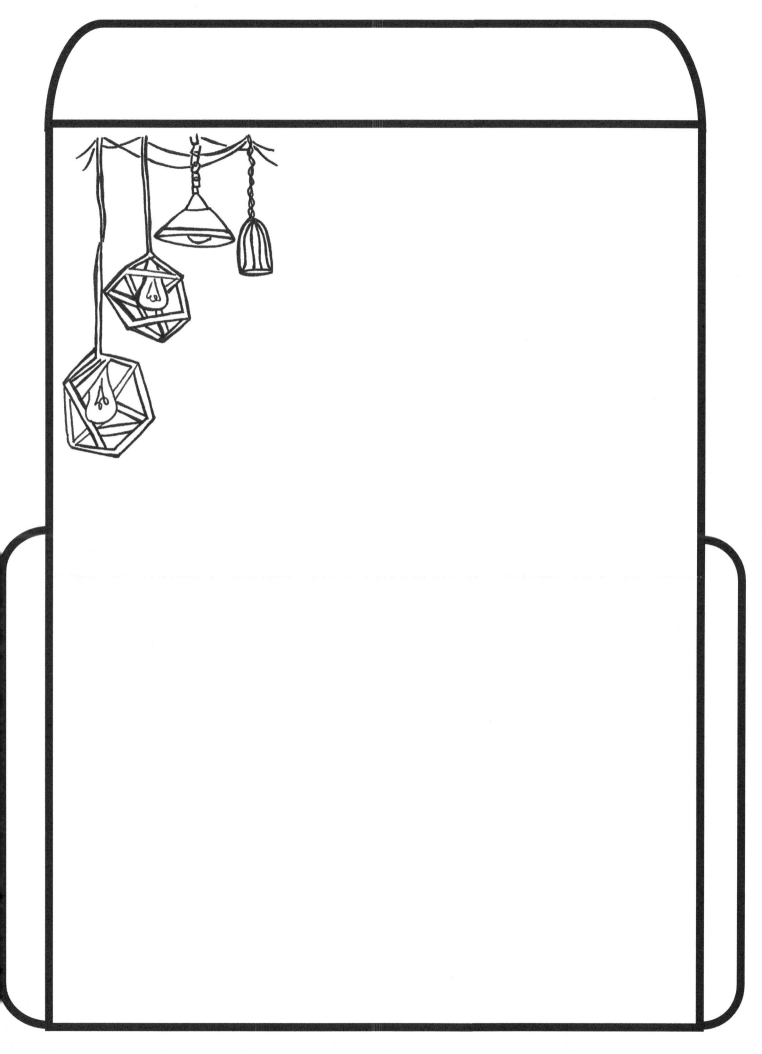

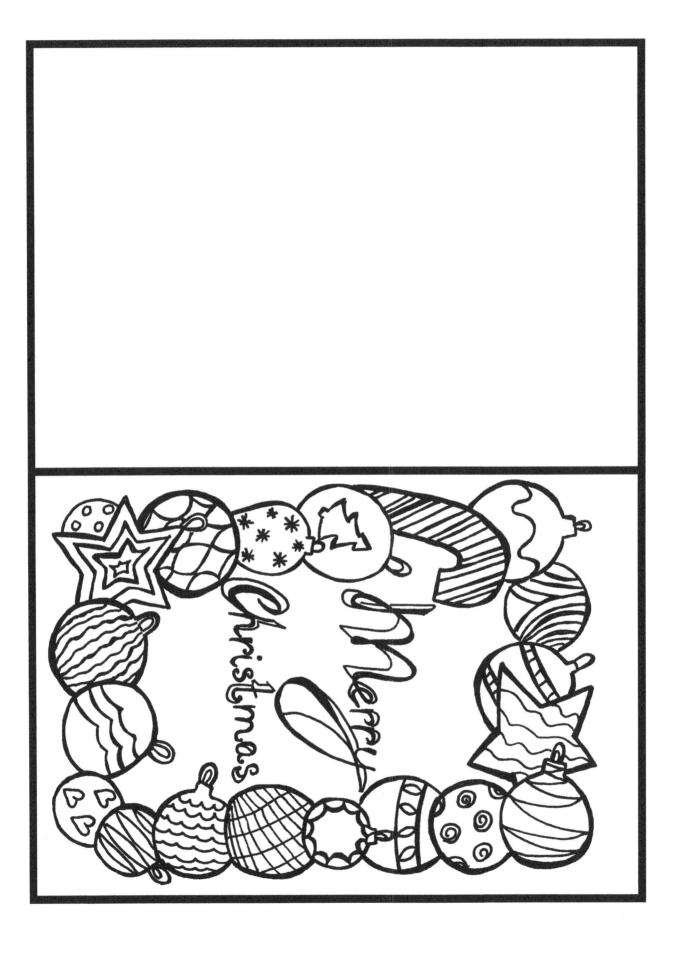

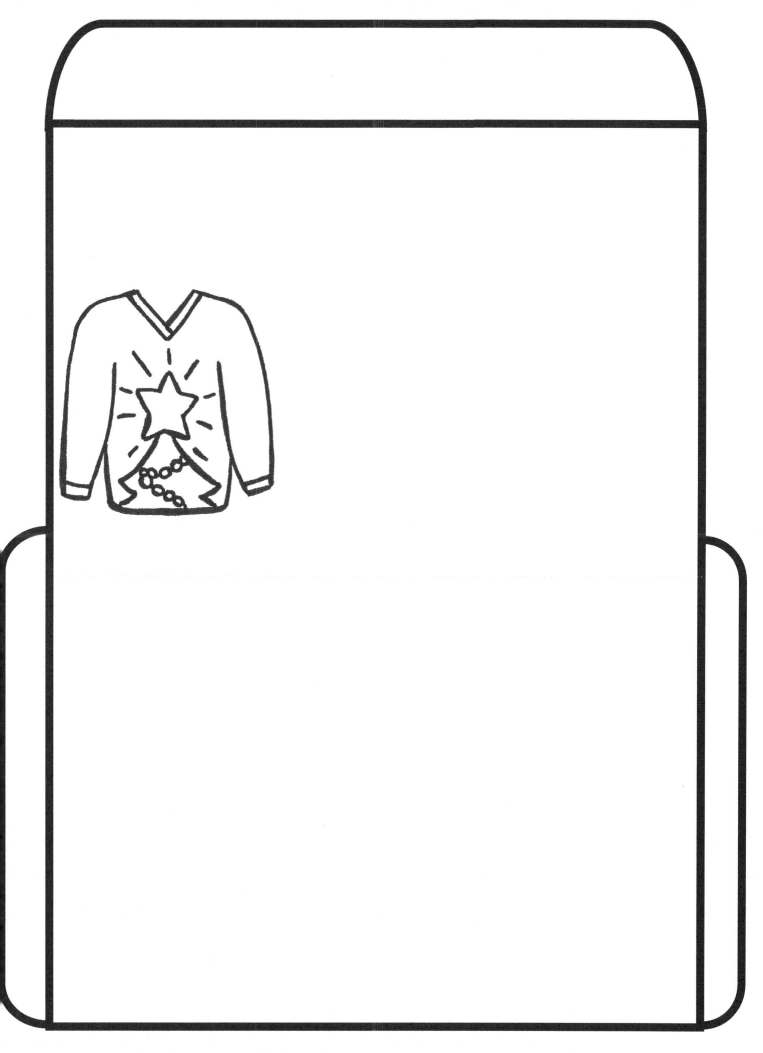

DESIGN YOUR OWN CARDS!

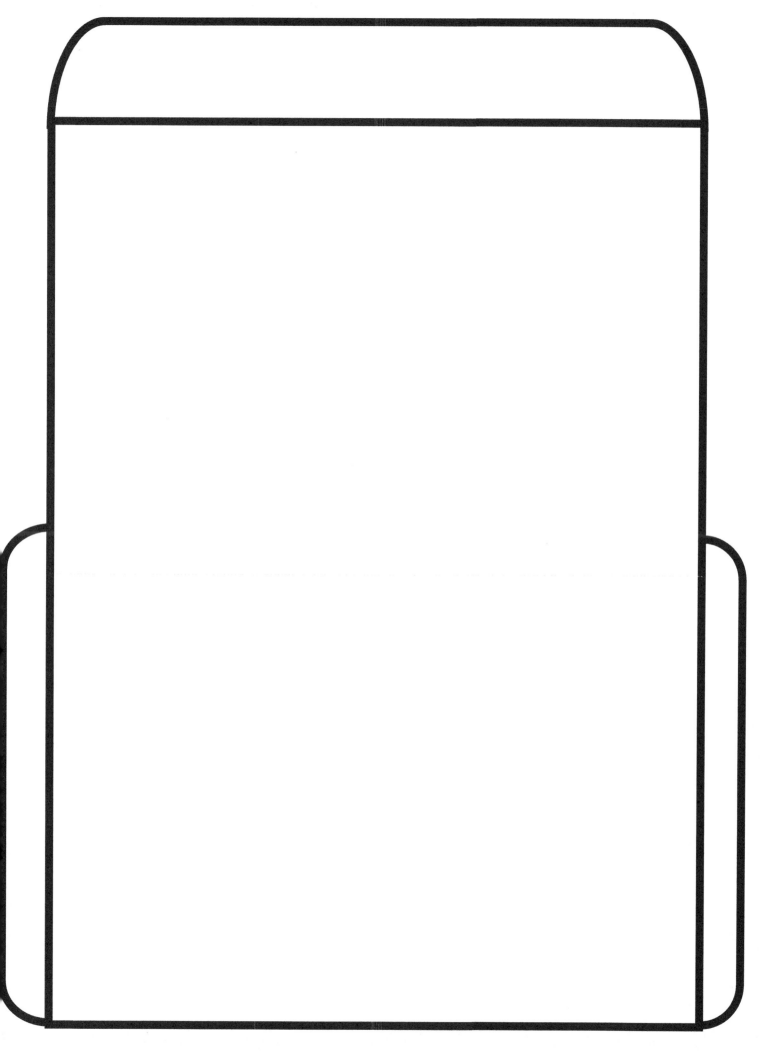

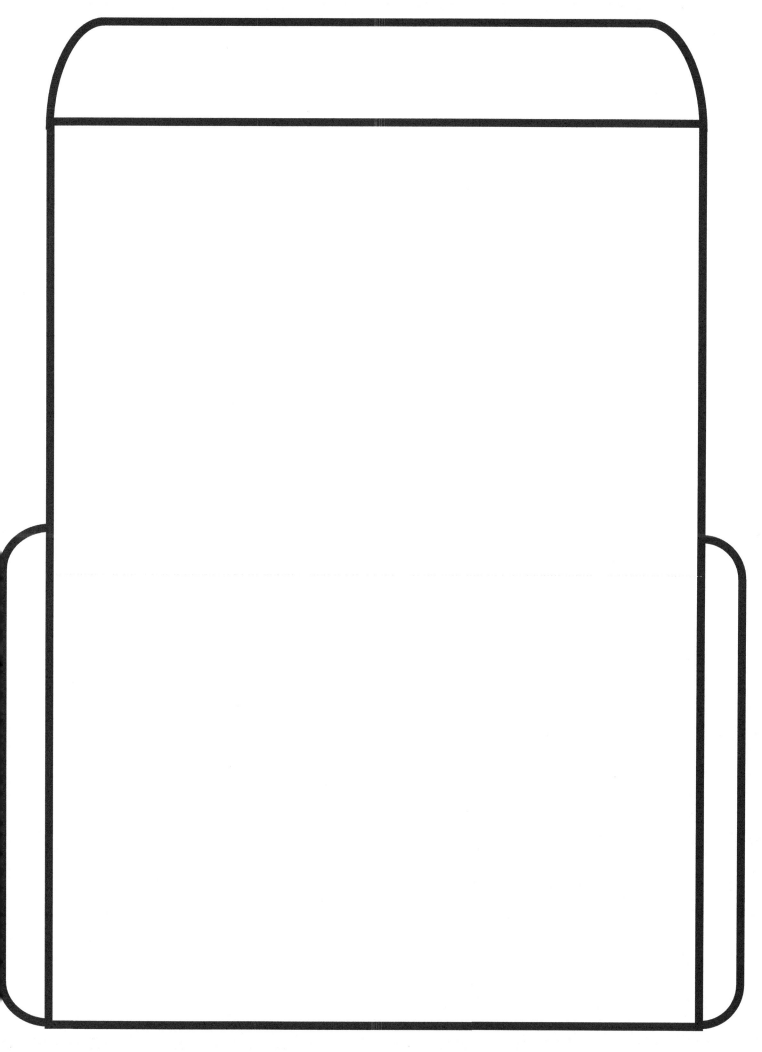

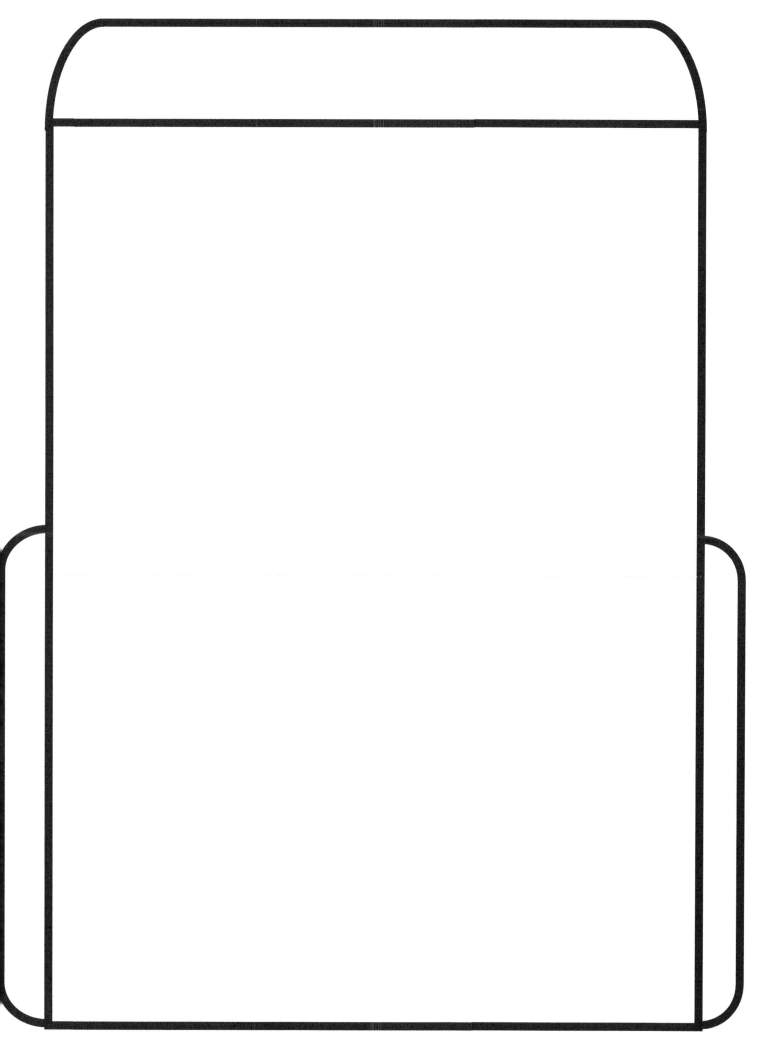

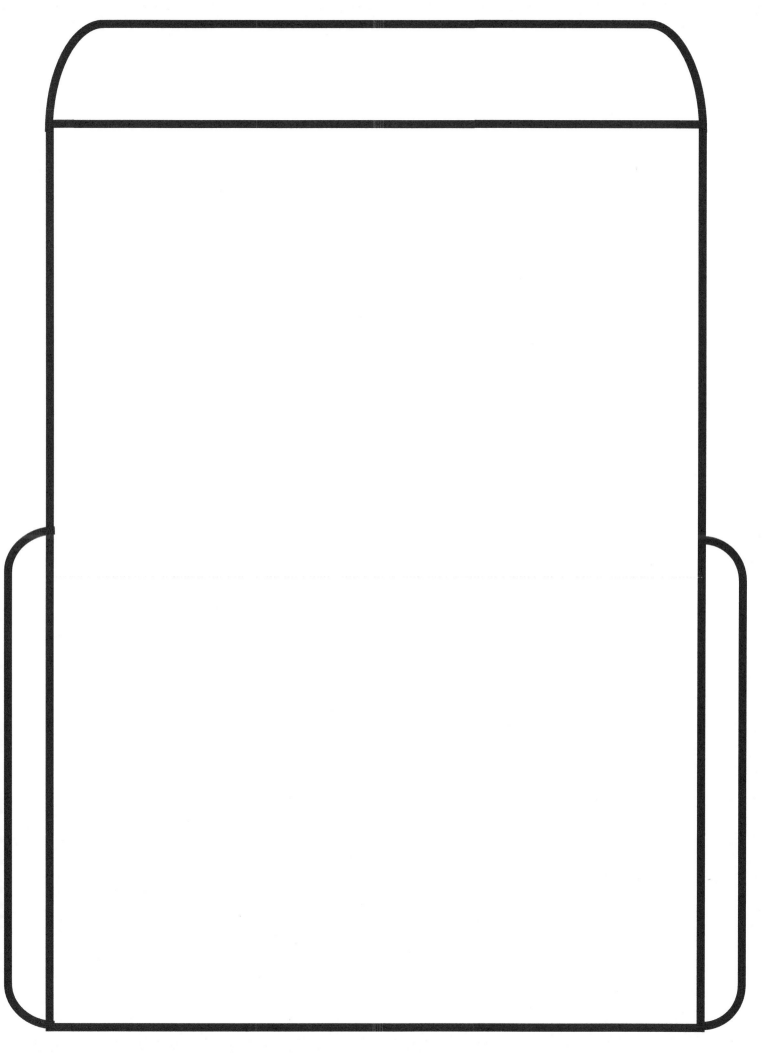

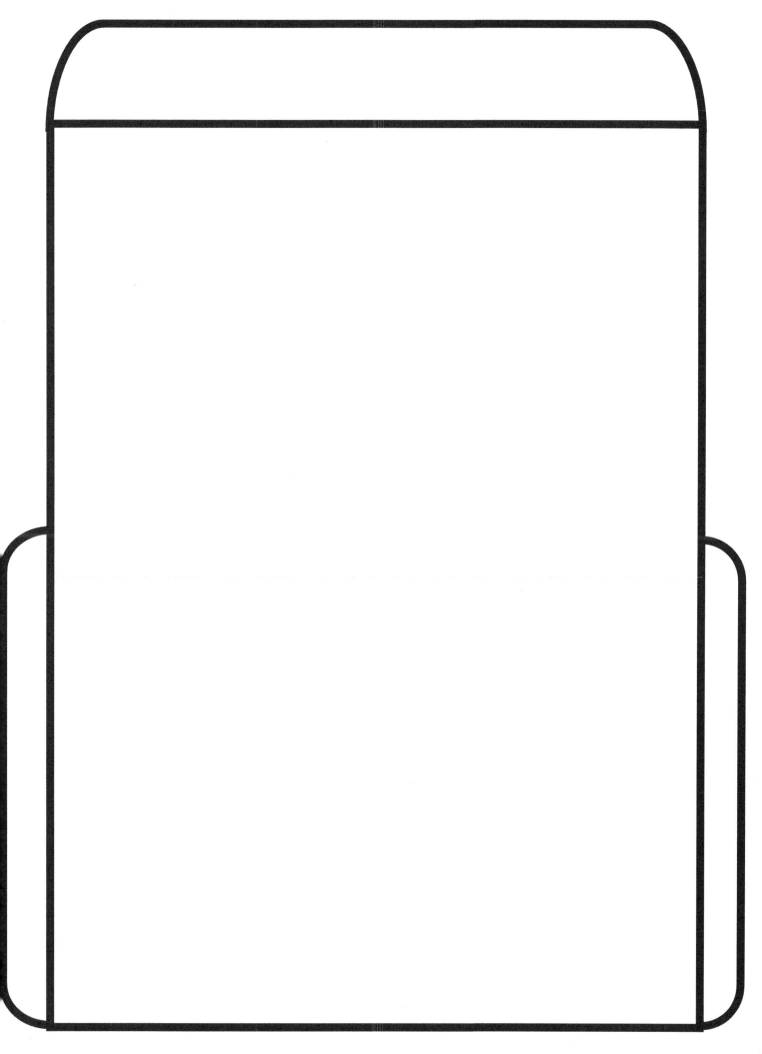

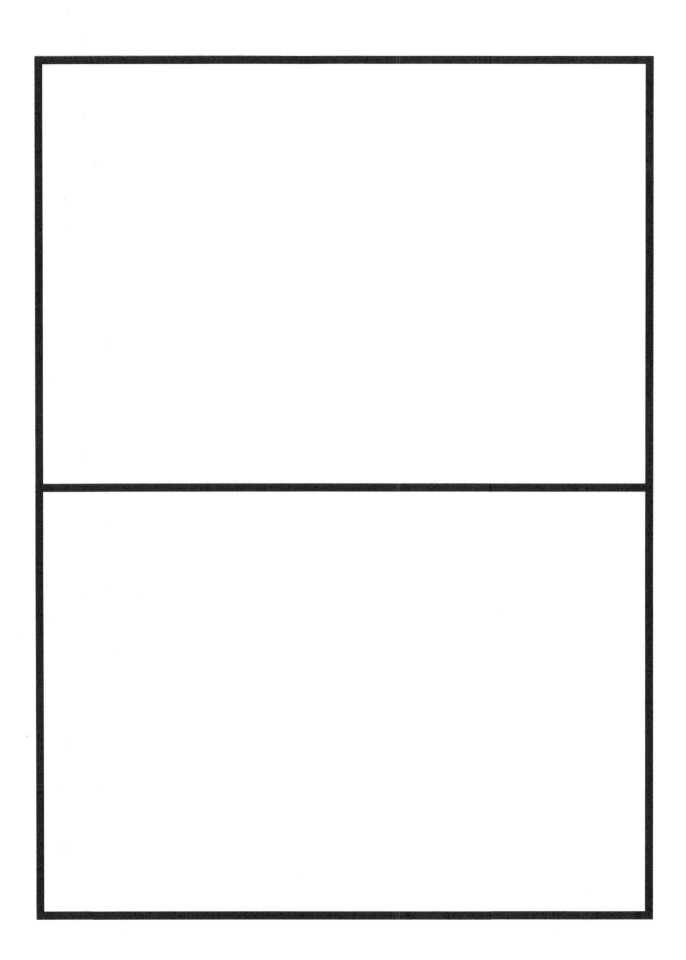

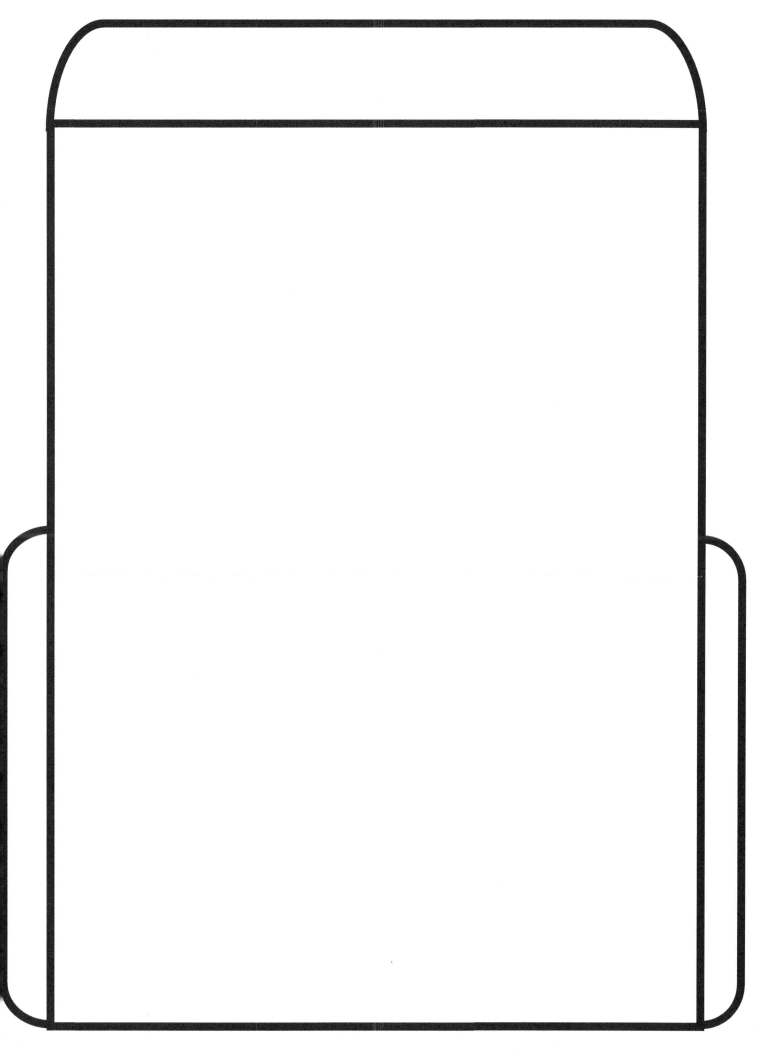

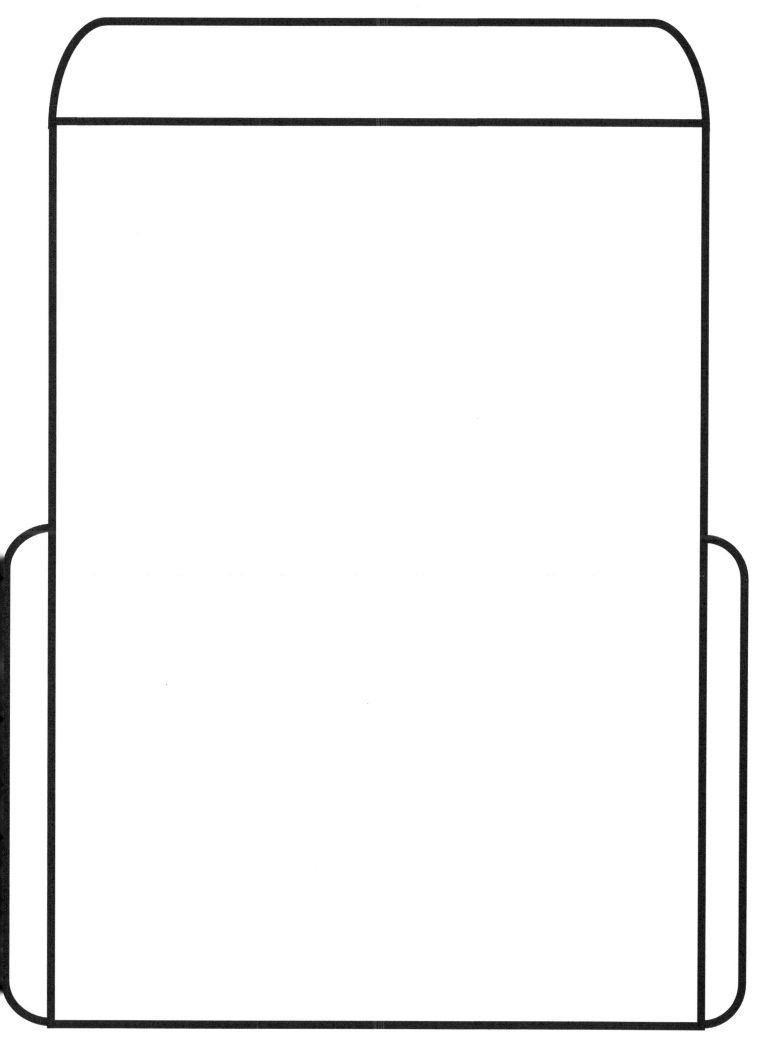

Made in the USA
Coppell, TX
08 April 2022